CLASSIC PIANO REPERTOIRE

CHRISTMAS

8 TRADITIONAL CAROLS

ARRANGED FOR SOLO PIANO

BY EDNA MAE BURNAM, WILLIAM GILLOCK,
JOHN THOMPSON AND GLENDA AUSTIN

ISBN 978-1-4768-1276-2

WILLIS MUSIC

EXCLUSIVELY DISTRIBUTED BY

HAL•LEONARD®
CORPORATION
7777 W. BLUEMOUND RD. P.O. BOX 13819 MILWAUKEE, WI 53213

Visit Hal Leonard Online at
www.halleonard.com

EDNA MAE BURNAM (1907–2007) is best known as the author of the best-selling *A Dozen a Day* books. The technique series with the iconic stick-figure drawings that Burnam herself drew has sold over 30 million copies worldwide. Burnam was born in Sacramento, California and began piano lessons at age 7 with her mother, Armilda Mae Will (also a piano teacher). She would go on to major in piano at the University of Washington and Chico State College, after which she set up her own private studio. Her long, productive association with Willis Music began when she signed her first royalty contract in 1937. She followed up the success of *A Dozen a Day* with the *Step by Step* piano course, and in her lifetime composed hundreds of individual songs and pieces, many based on whimsical subjects she encountered during her travels.

The two Christmas tunes included in this collection are from *My Christmas Carol Book*, first published in 1956.

WILLIAM GILLOCK's (1917–1993) fame as a composer rests arguably on his affinity for romantic melody and structure. Often referred to as the "Schubert of children's composers," Gillock was born in a small town in Missouri and was a graduate of Central Methodist University. His musical career led him to long tenures in New Orleans and Dallas, where he was always in high demand as a teacher, clinician, and composer. Some of Gillock's most popular publications include the *New Orleans Jazz Styles* series, the dazzling solo piece "Fountain in the Rain," and the *Accent on Solos* repertoire series.

The Christmas arrangements included in this book are from the 1968 collection, *Christmas at the Piano.*

JOHN THOMPSON (1889–1963) was 10 years of age when the Willis Music Company was established in Cincinnati, Ohio. A few years later, his lifelong collaboration with Willis would begin. Thompson began his distinguished musical career as a young concert pianist and performed to great reviews in major venues in the United States and Europe. After his concert career ended, he became a respected piano pedagogue, heading music conservatories in his hometown of Philadelphia as well as in Indianapolis and Kansas City. It was during these tenures that he developed original ideas about teaching young children and adults. His best-selling method books *Teaching Little Fingers to Play* and *Modern Course for the Piano* were first published by the Willis Music Company in the mid-1930s and soon grew to include the Easiest Piano Course and several other notable educational publications. To this day, these methods remain incredibly popular throughout the world.

The Thompson arrangements in this book were originally part of *The John Thompson Book of Christmas Carols*, first published in 1960.

GLENDA AUSTIN (b.1951) first contacted William Gillock in 1980, as a musician and teacher, and as an enthusiastic admirer of his music. She also had questions about composing and publishing her own music. Gillock responded warmly, and the correspondence between the two Missouri natives developed into a close and supportive friendship that lasted until Gillock's death in 1993. Because of this connection, Austin was selected by Willis Music to arrange Gillock's popular *New Orleans Jazz Styles* series, first into a simplified version and more recently into duets. Austin was born and raised in Joplin, Missouri and received her music education and piano performance degrees from the University of Missouri (Columbia). She currently teaches choral and general music classes in Joplin and is an adjunct faculty member of Missouri Southern State University.

The arrangements in this compilation are part of her *Christmas Classics* series (1995).

FROM THE PUBLISHERS

The *Classic Piano Repertoire* series includes popular as well as lesser-known pieces from a select group of composers out of the Willis piano archives (established in 1899). This special volume features eight Christmas carol arrangements by Edna Mae Burnam, William Gillock, John Thompson and Glenda Austin, and the pieces range from early to later elementary. Each piece has been newly engraved and edited with the aim to preserve each composer's original intent and musical purpose.

CONTENTS

Jingle Bells

Jingle bells! Jingle bells! Jingle all the way!
Oh, what fun it is to ride in a one-horse open sleigh!

By J. Pierpont
Arranged by Glenda Austin

Happily, with a bounce (In 2)

© 1995 by The Willis Music Co.
International Copyright Secured   All Rights Reserved

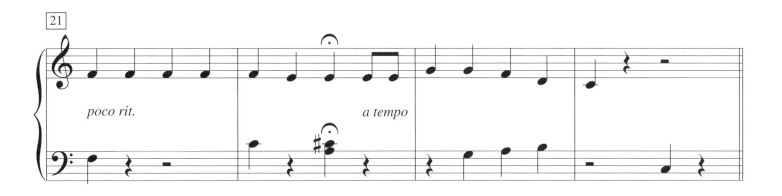

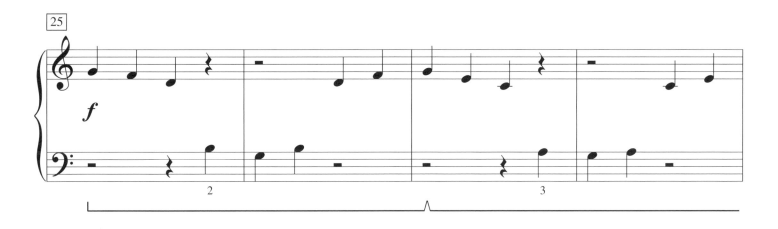

Jolly Old Saint Nicholas

Jolly old Saint Nicholas, lean your ear this way!
Don't you tell a single soul what I'm going to say.
Christmas Eve is coming soon; now, you dear old man,
Whisper what you'll bring to me, tell me, if you can.

19th Century American Carol
Arranged by Edna Mae Burnam

Deck the Hall

Deck the halls with boughs of holly, fa la la...
Tis the season to be jolly, fa la la...
Don we now our gay apparel, fa la la...
Troll the ancient Yuletide carol, fa la la....

Traditional Welsh Carol
Arranged by John Thompson

God Rest You Merry, Gentlemen

God rest you merry, gentlemen, let nothing you dismay,
Remember Christ our Saviour was born on Christmas day,
To save us all from Satan's pow'r when we were gone astray;
O tidings of comfort and joy, comfort and joy,
O tidings of comfort and joy.

English
Arranged by William Gillock

Moderately, with a slightly solemn feel

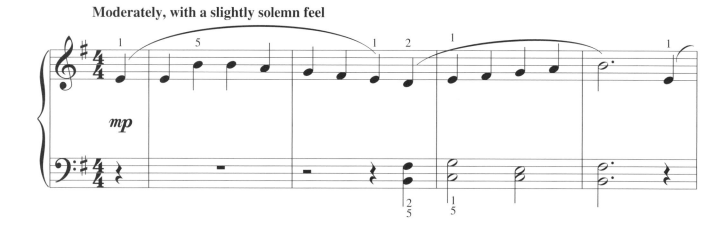

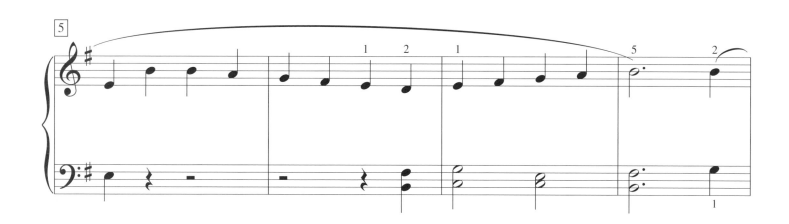

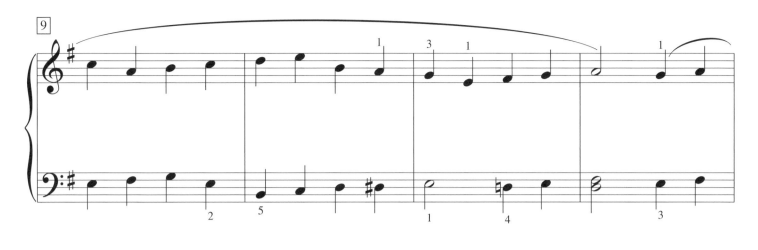

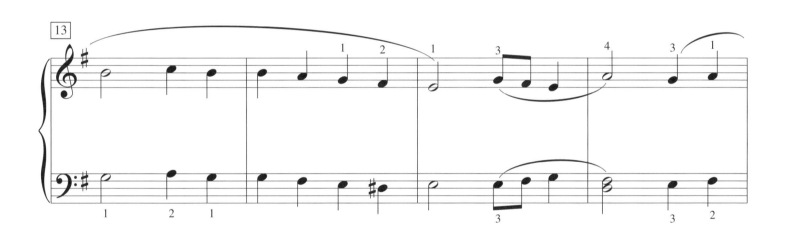

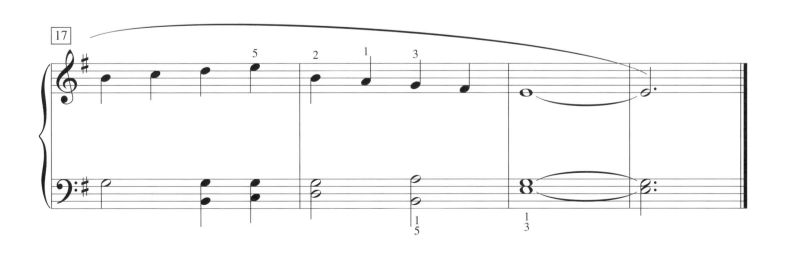

Silent Night

Silent night, holy night.
All is calm, all is bright.
Round yon virgin mother and child,
Holy infant so tender and mild.
Sleep in heavenly peace.

By Franz Gruber
Arranged by William Gillock

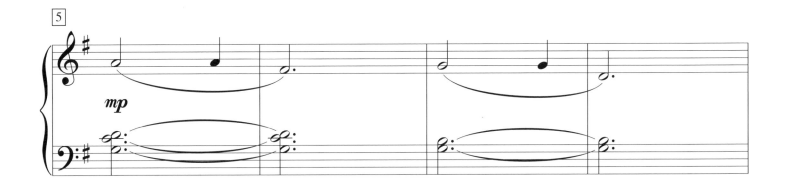

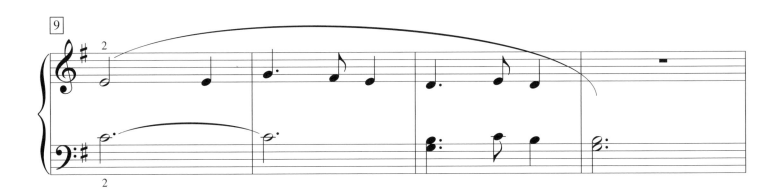

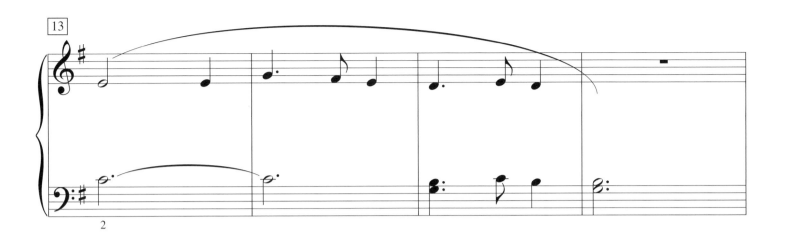

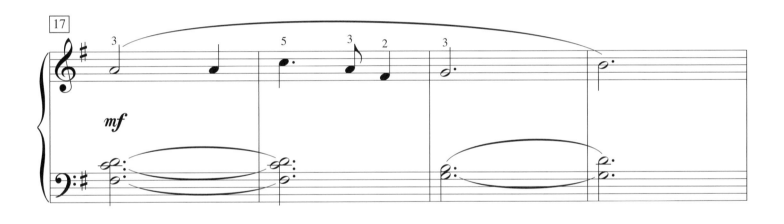

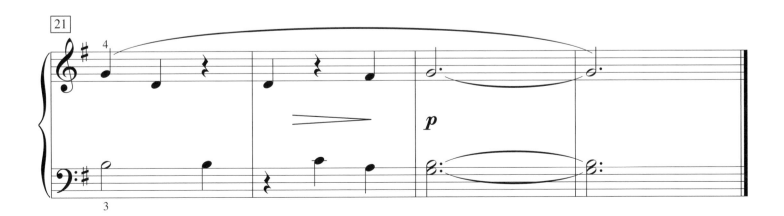

It Came Upon the Midnight Clear

It came upon the midnight clear, that glorious song of old,
From angels bending near the earth to touch their harps of gold:
"Peace on the earth, good will to men, from heav'n's all-gracious King."
The world in solemn stillness lay to hear the angels sing.

Words by Edmund Hamilton Sears
Music by Richard Storrs Willis
Arranged by John Thompson

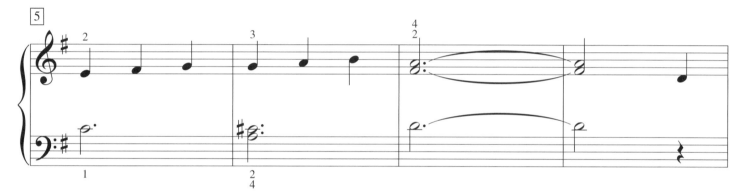

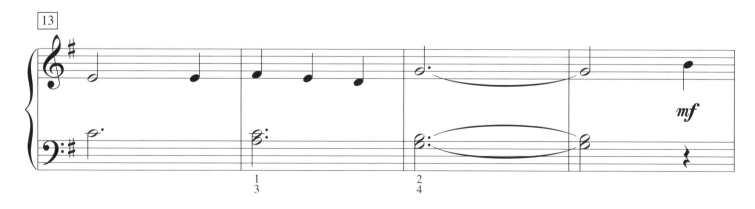

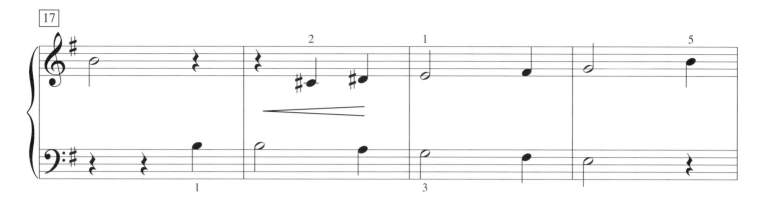

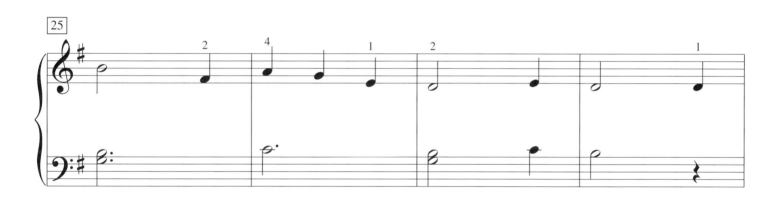

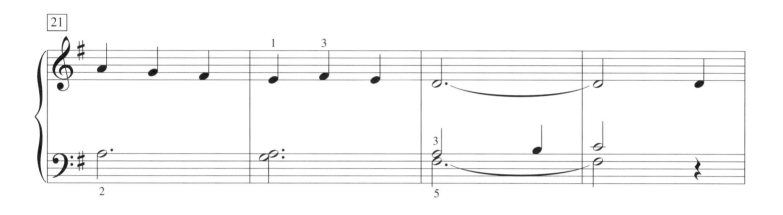

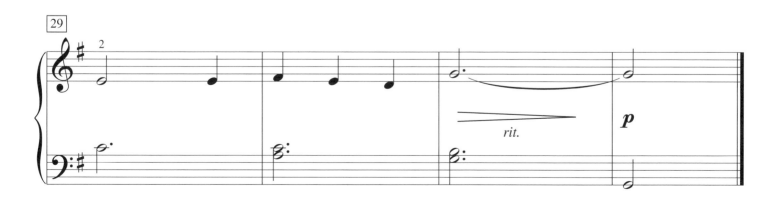

O Little Town of Bethlehem

O little town of Bethlehem, how still we see thee lie;
Above the deep and dreamless sleep the silent stars go by.
Yet in thy dark streets shineth the everlasting light.
The hopes and fears of all the years are met in thee tonight.

Words by Phillips Brooks
Music by Lewis H. Redner
Arranged by Glenda Austin

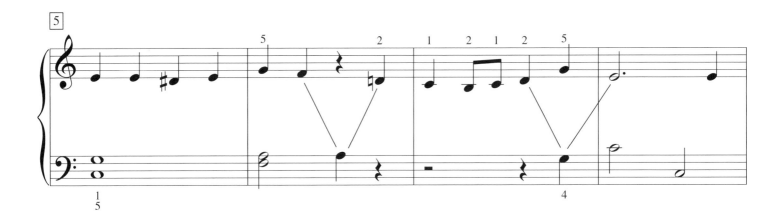

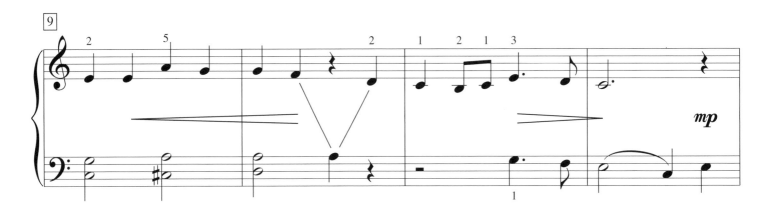

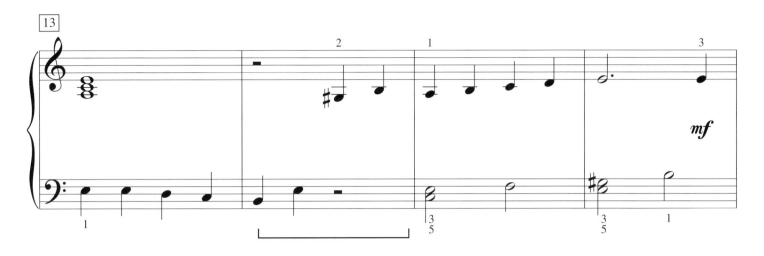

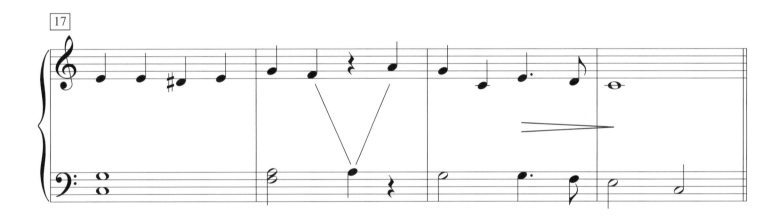

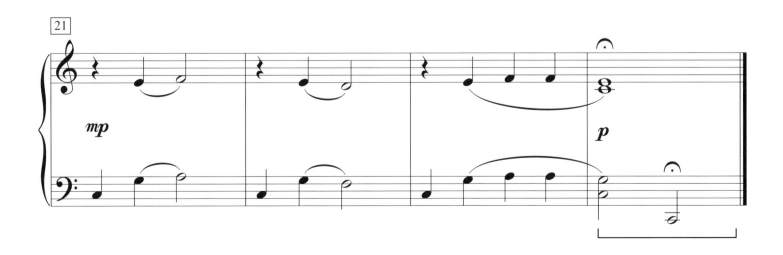

O Come, Little Children

O come, little children, O come, one and all!
O come to the cradle in Bethlehem's stall!
Come, look in the manger! There sleeps on the hay
An infant so lovely in light bright as day.

Words by Christoph von Schmid
Music by J.P.A. Schulz
Arranged by Edna Mae Burnam